remembering

Concert Memories

the good times

You've just attended the most awesome
concert ever. You'll remember it forever.
Except that you won't.
Journal it and never forget!

Concert:

Ticket

Date:

Venue/Seat:

Rating:

Who I was with: _____

_____

_____

Awesomeness: _____

_____

_____

_____

Play List: _____

_____

_____

_____

_____

_____

_____

_____

Concert:

Ticket

Date:

Venue/Seat:

Rating:

Who I was with: _____

_____

_____

Awesomeness: _____

_____

_____

_____

Play List: _____

_____

_____

_____

_____

_____

_____

_____

_____

Concert:

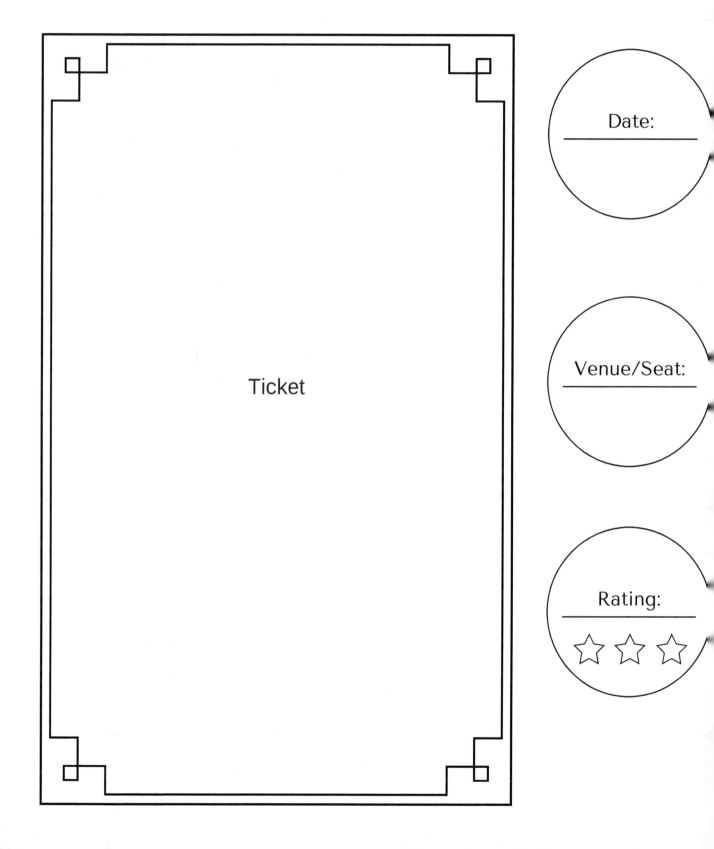

Ticket

Date:

Venue/Seat:

Rating:

Who I was with: _____

_____

_____

Awesomeness: _____

_____

_____

_____

Play List: _____

_____

_____

_____

_____

_____

_____

_____

Concert:

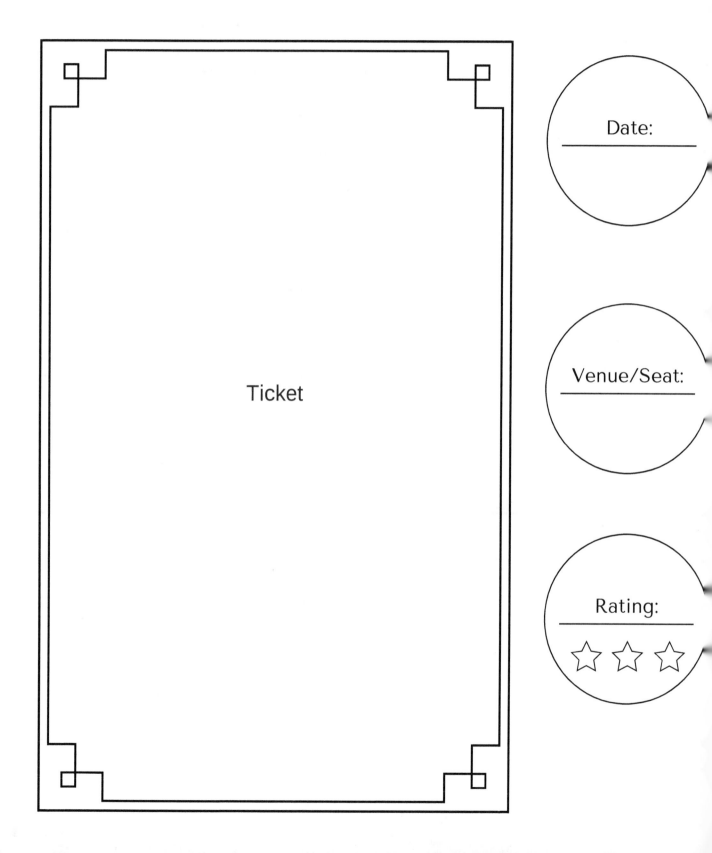

Ticket

Date:

Venue/Seat:

Rating:

Who I was with: _____

_____

_____

Awesomeness: _____

_____

_____

Play List: _____

_____

_____

_____

_____

_____

_____

_____

Concert:

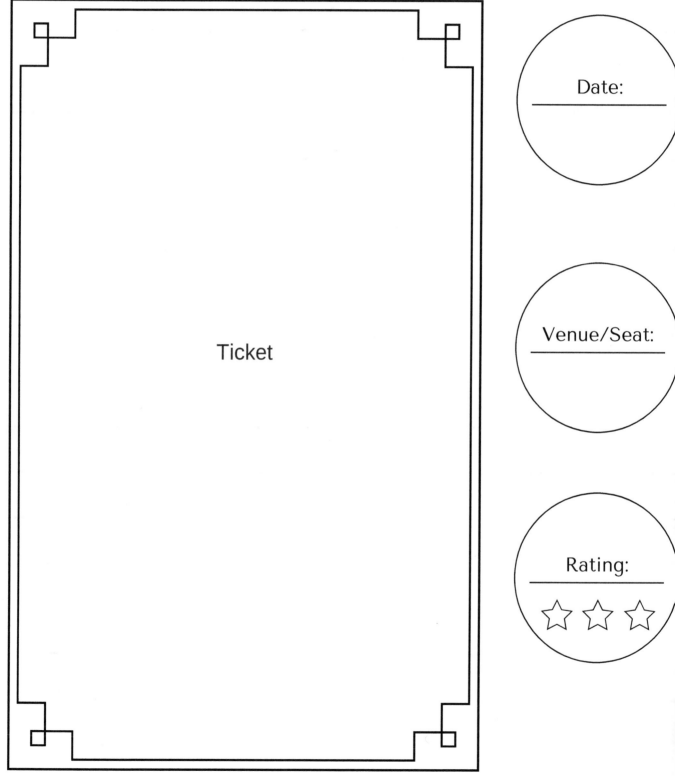

Ticket

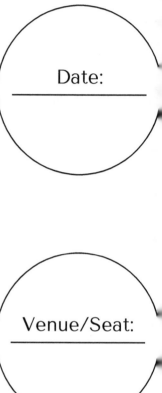

Date:

Venue/Seat:

Rating:

Who I was with: _____

_____

_____

Awesomeness: _____

_____

_____

_____

Play List: _____

_____

_____

_____

_____

_____

_____

_____

Concert:

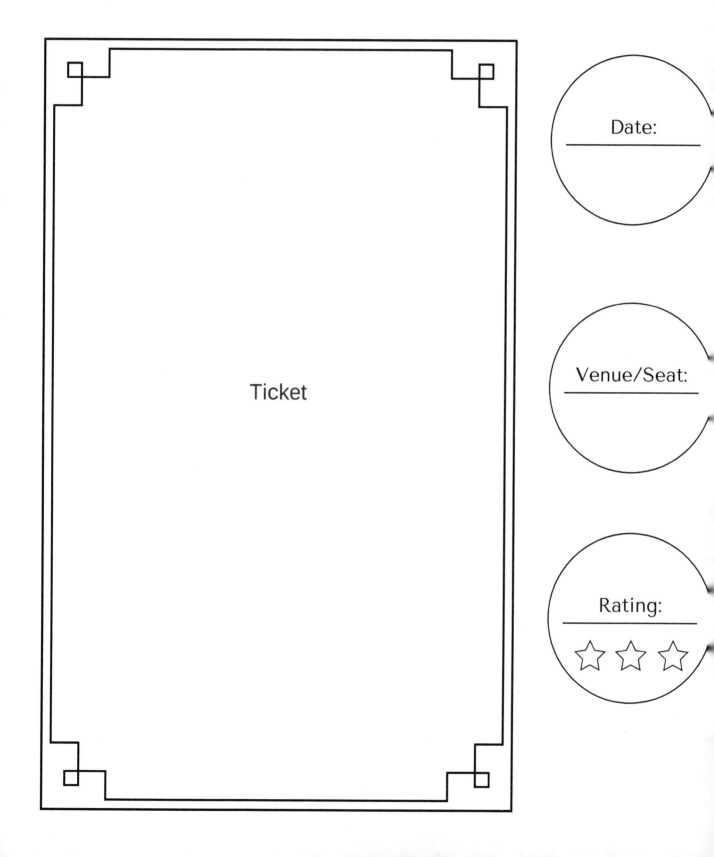

Ticket

Date:

Venue/Seat:

Rating:

Who I was with: _____

_____

_____

Awesomeness: _____

_____

_____

_____

Play List: _____

_____

_____

_____

_____

_____

_____

_____

Concert:

Ticket

Date:

Venue/Seat:

Rating:

Who I was with: _____

_____

_____

Awesomeness: _____

_____

_____

_____

Play List: _____

_____

_____

_____

_____

_____

_____

_____

_____

Concert:

Ticket

Date:

Venue/Seat:

Rating:

Who I was with: _____

_____

_____

Awesomeness: _____

_____

_____

_____

Play List: _____

_____

_____

_____

_____

_____

_____

_____

_____

Concert:

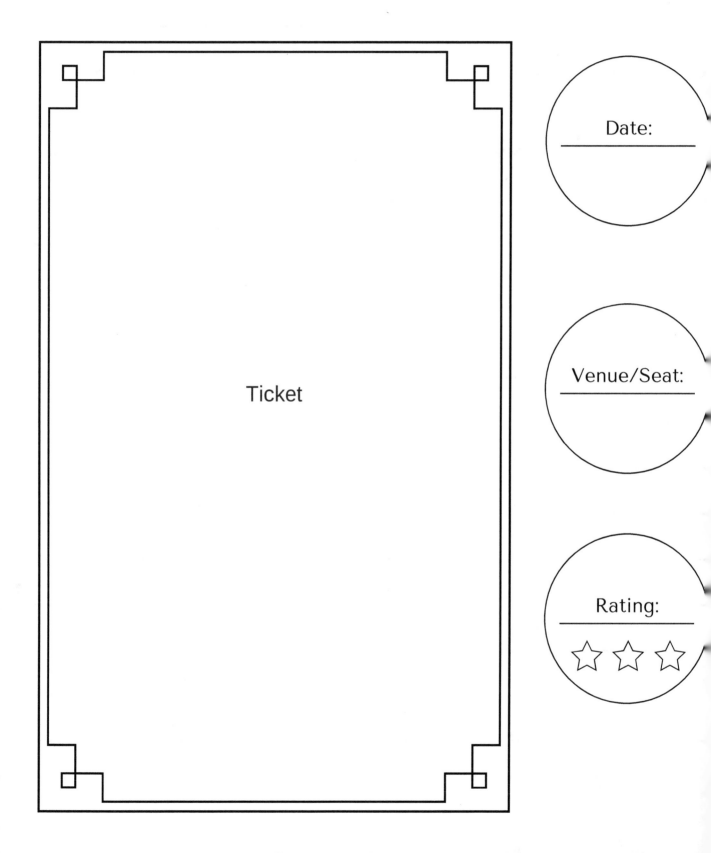

Ticket

Date:
_____

Venue/Seat:
_____

Rating:
_____
☆ ☆ ☆

Who I was with: _____

_____

_____

Awesomeness: _____

_____

_____

_____

Play List: _____

_____

_____

_____

_____

_____

_____

_____

_____

Concert:

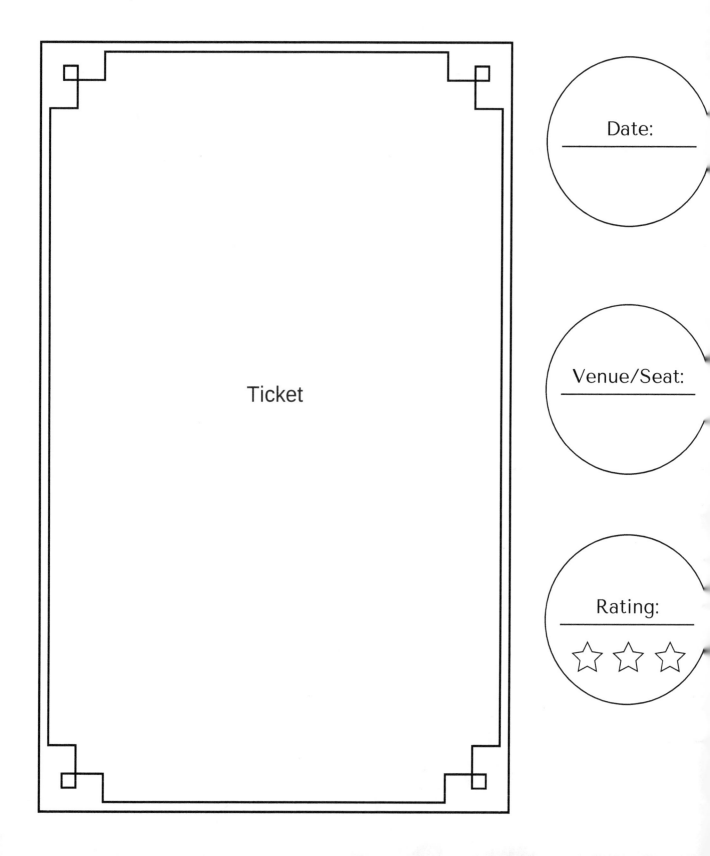

Ticket

Date:

Venue/Seat:

Rating:

Who I was with: _____

_____

_____

Awesomeness: _____

_____

_____

_____

Play List: _____

_____

_____

_____

_____

_____

_____

_____

_____

Concert:

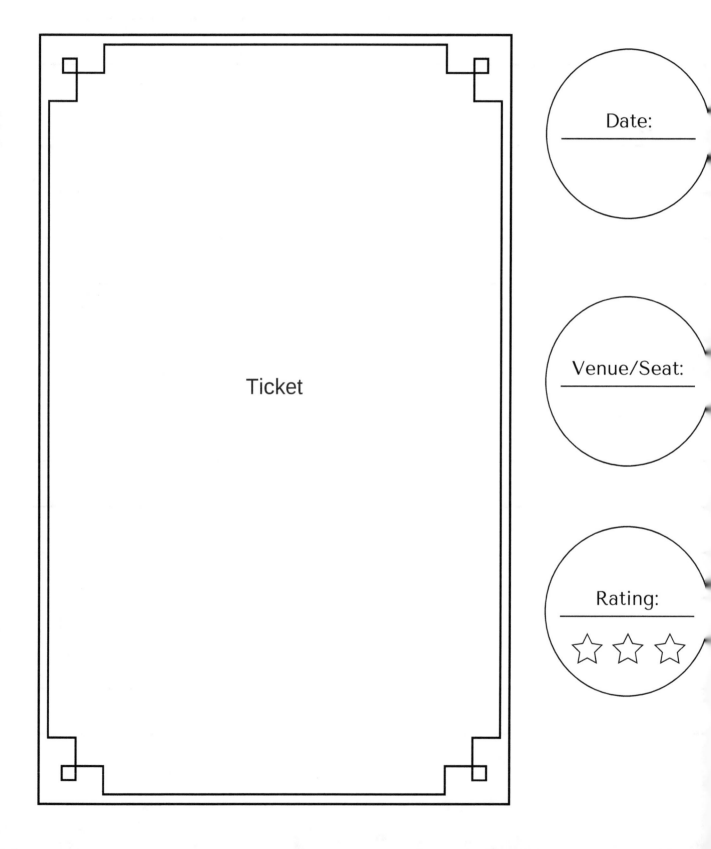

Ticket

Date:

Venue/Seat:

Rating:

Who I was with: _____

_____

_____

Awesomeness: _____

_____

_____

_____

Play List: _____

_____

_____

_____

_____

_____

_____

_____

Concert:

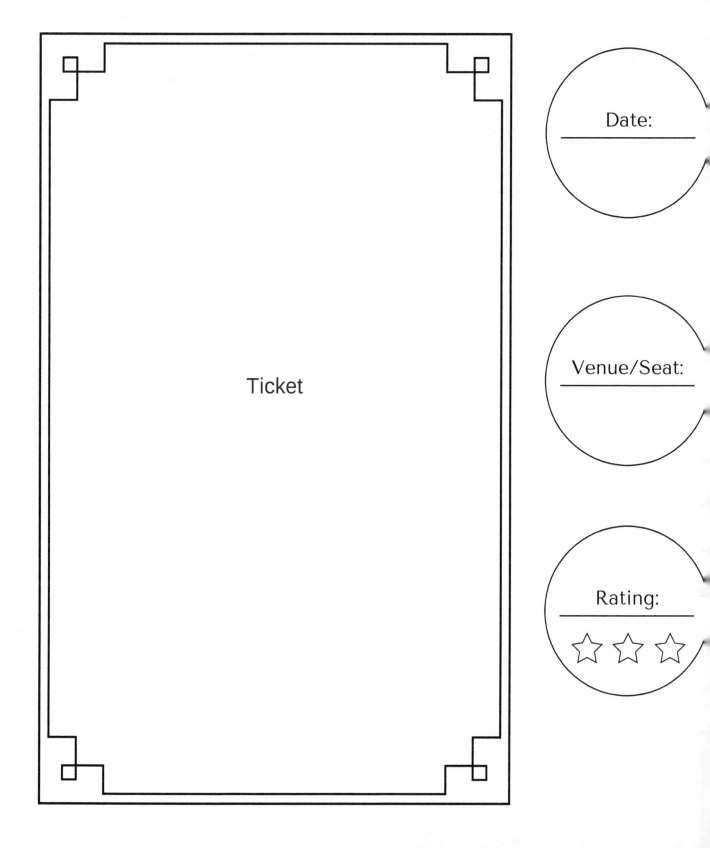

Ticket

Date:

Venue/Seat:

Rating:

Who I was with: _____

_____

_____

Awesomeness: _____

_____

_____

_____

Play List: _____

_____

_____

_____

_____

_____

_____

_____

Concert:

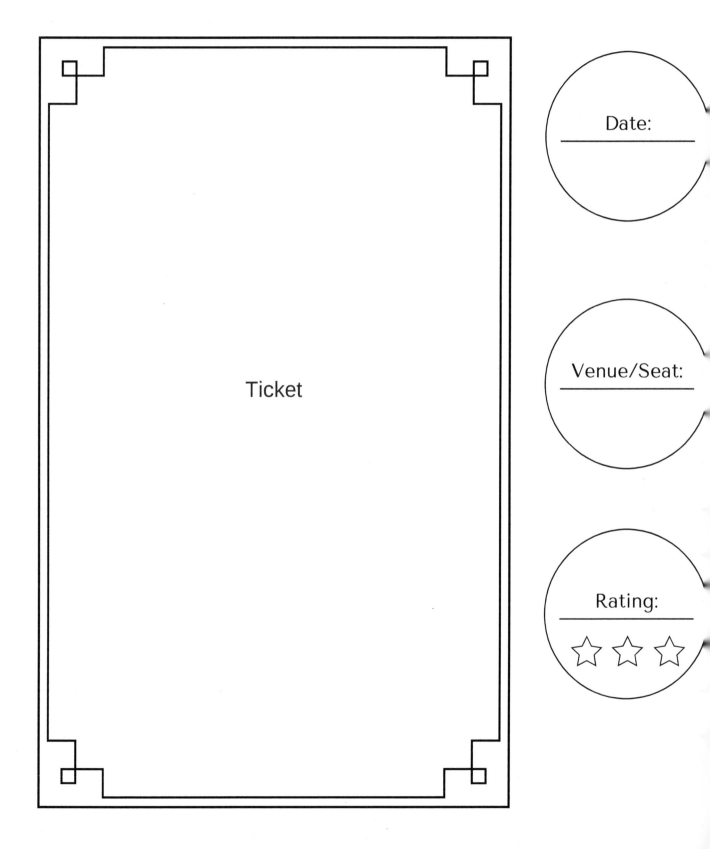

Ticket

Date:

Venue/Seat:

Rating:

Who I was with: _____

_____

_____

Awesomeness: _____

_____

_____

_____

Play List: _____

_____

_____

_____

_____

_____

_____

_____

Concert:

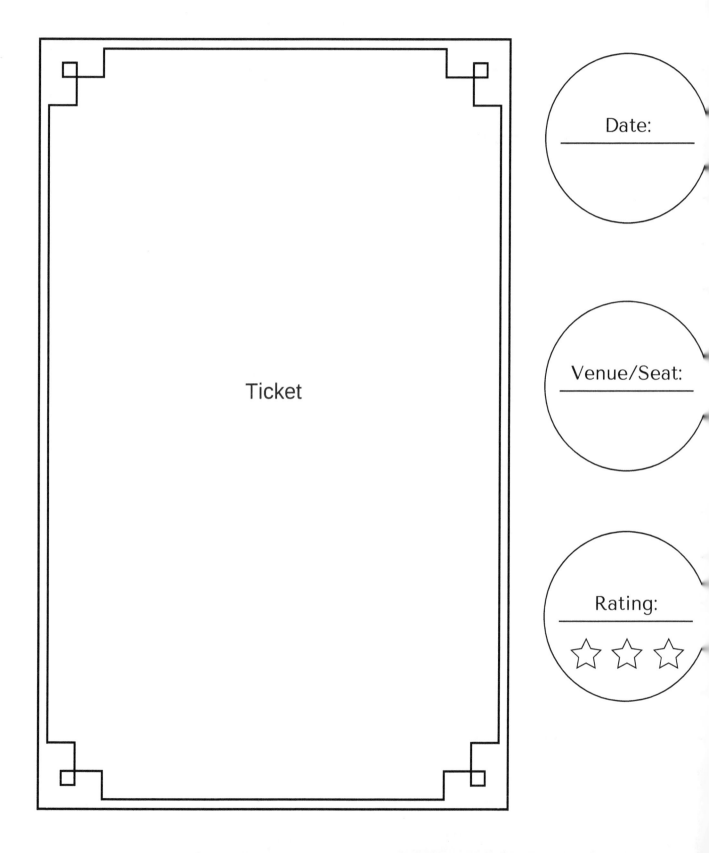

Ticket

Date:

Venue/Seat:

Rating:

Who I was with: _____

_____

_____

Awesomeness: _____

_____

_____

_____

Play List: _____

_____

_____

_____

_____

_____

_____

Favorite Memories

Favorite Concert Venue:

_____

_____

_____

_____

_____

Favorite Concert Food:

_____

_____

_____

_____

_____

Favorite Concert So Far:

_____

_____

_____

_____

_____

Best Concert Experience So Far:

_____

_____

_____

_____

_____

_____

_____

_____

_____

_____

_____

_____

Concert:

Ticket

Date:

Venue/Seat:

Rating:

Who I was with: _____

_____

_____

Awesomeness: _____

_____

_____

_____

Play List: _____

_____

_____

_____

_____

_____

_____

_____

Concert:

Ticket

Date:

Venue/Seat:

Rating:

Who I was with: _____

_____

_____

Awesomeness: _____

_____

_____

_____

Play List: _____

_____

_____

_____

_____

_____

_____

_____

Concert:

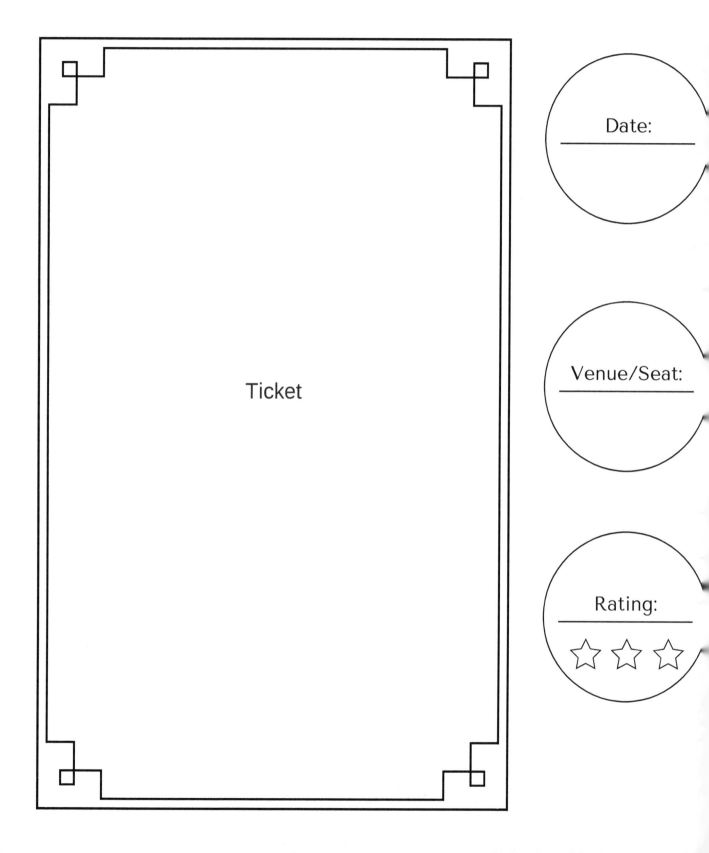

Ticket

Date:

Venue/Seat:

Rating:

Who I was with: _____

_____

_____

Awesomeness: _____

_____

_____

_____

Play List: _____

_____

_____

_____

_____

_____

_____

_____

Concert:

Ticket

Date:

Venue/Seat:

Rating:

Who I was with: _____

_____

_____

Awesomeness: _____

_____

_____

_____

Play List: _____

_____

_____

_____

_____

_____

_____

_____

Concert:

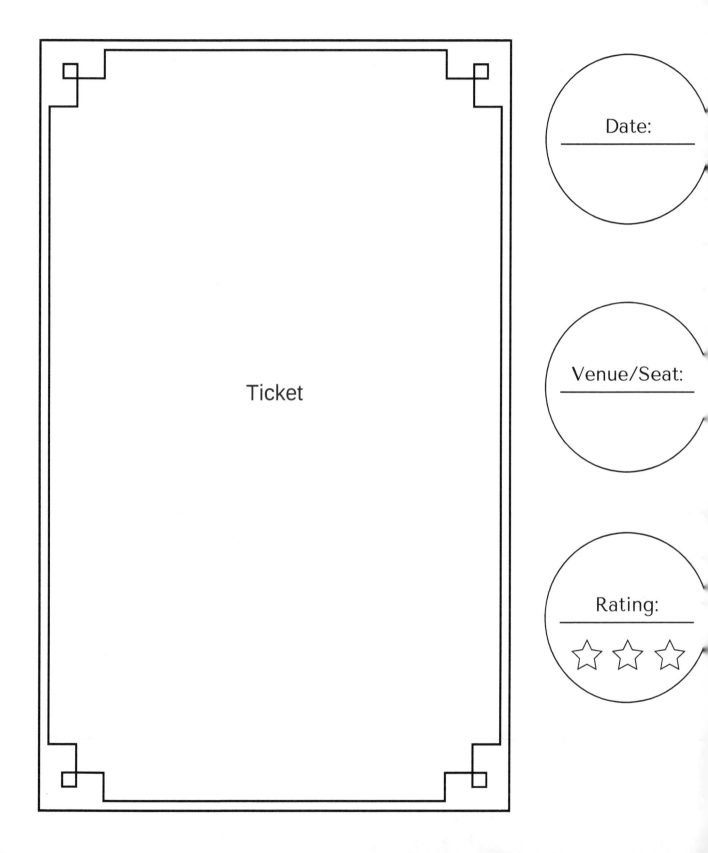

Ticket

Date:

Venue/Seat:

Rating:

Who I was with: _____

_____

_____

Awesomeness: _____

_____

_____

_____

Play List: _____

_____

_____

_____

_____

_____

_____

_____

Concert:

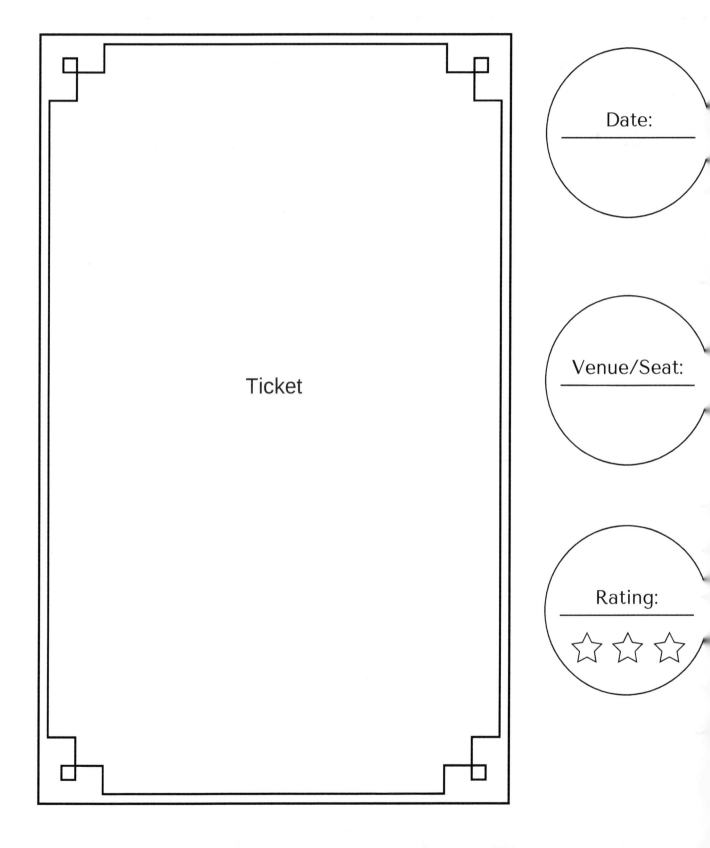

Ticket

Date:

Venue/Seat:

Rating:

Who I was with: _____

_____

_____

Awesomeness: _____

_____

_____

_____

Play List: _____

_____

_____

_____

_____

_____

_____

_____

_____

Concert:

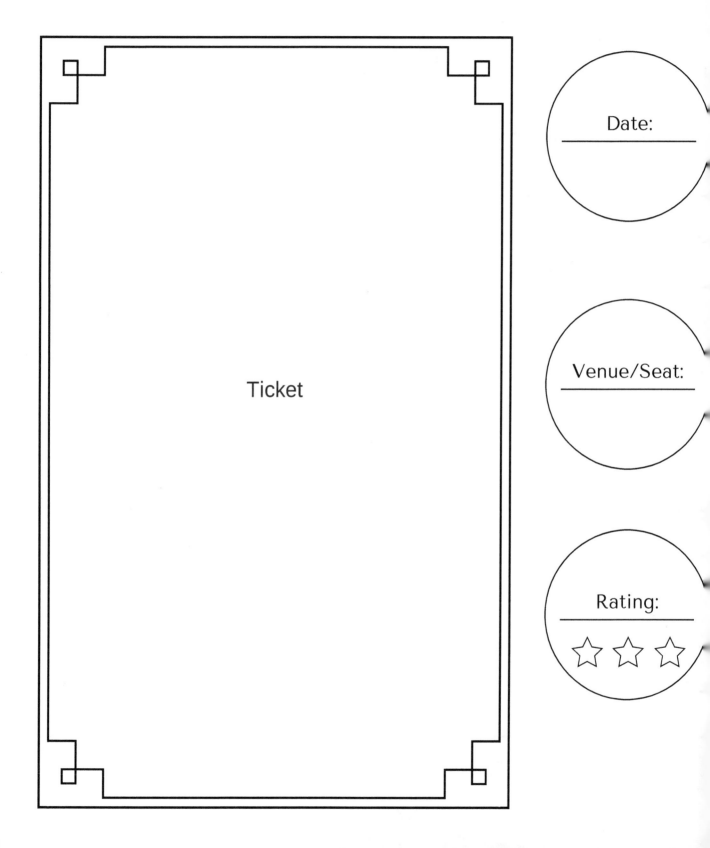

Ticket

Date:

Venue/Seat:

Rating:

Who I was with: _____

_____

_____

Awesomeness: _____

_____

_____

_____

Play List: _____

_____

_____

_____

_____

_____

_____

_____

_____

Concert:

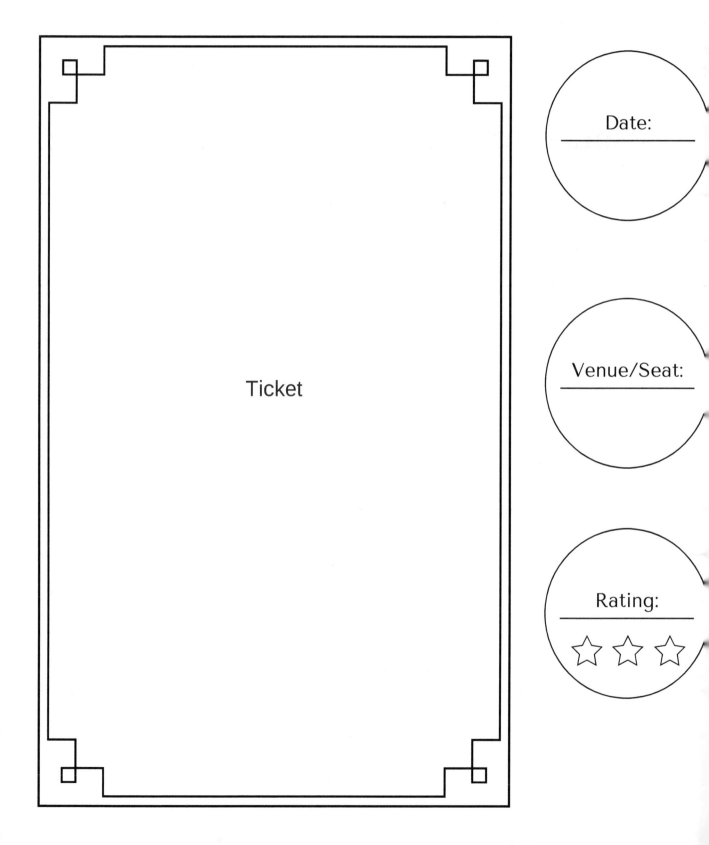

Ticket

Date:

Venue/Seat:

Rating:

Who I was with: _____

_____

_____

Awesomeness: _____

_____

_____

_____

Play List: _____

_____

_____

_____

_____

_____

_____

_____

_____

Concert:

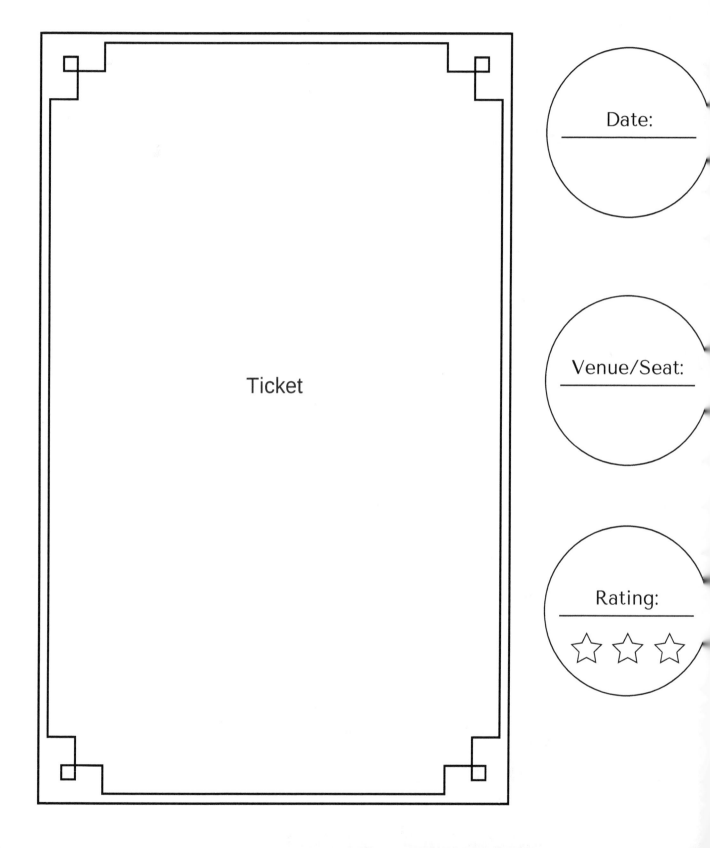

Ticket

Date:

Venue/Seat:

Rating:

Who I was with: _____

_____

_____

Awesomeness: _____

_____

_____

_____

Play List: _____

_____

_____

_____

_____

_____

_____

_____

Concert:

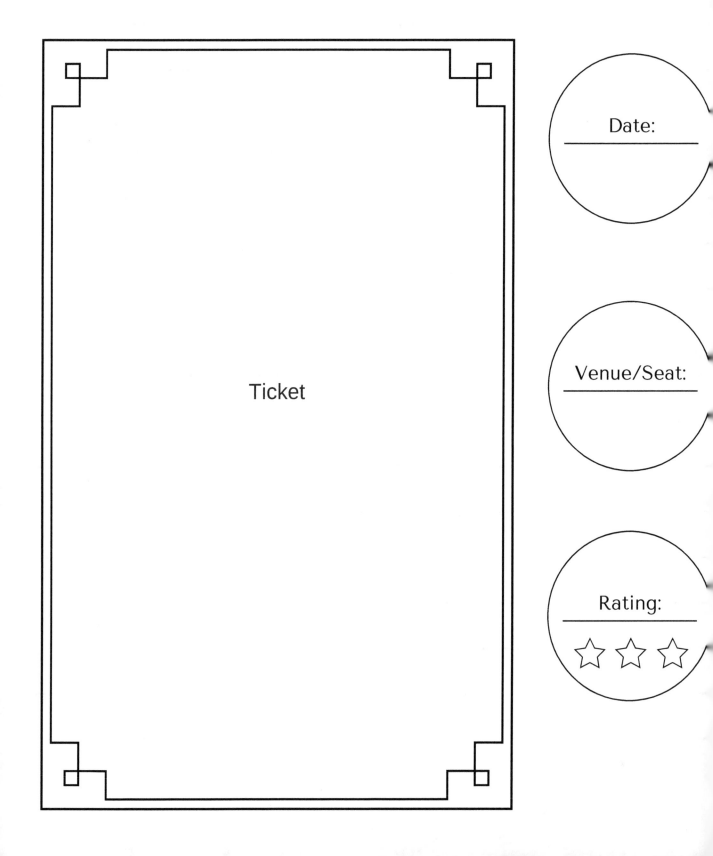

Ticket

Date:

Venue/Seat:

Rating:

Who I was with: _____

_____

_____

Awesomeness: _____

_____

_____

_____

Play List: _____

_____

_____

_____

_____

_____

_____

_____

_____

Concert:

Ticket

Date:

Venue/Seat:

Rating:

Who I was with: _____

_____

_____

Awesomeness: _____

_____

_____

_____

Play List: _____

_____

_____

_____

_____

_____

_____

_____

_____

Concert:

Ticket

Date:

Venue/Seat:

Rating:

Who I was with: _____

_____

_____

Awesomeness: _____

_____

_____

_____

Play List: _____

_____

_____

_____

_____

_____

_____

_____

Concert:

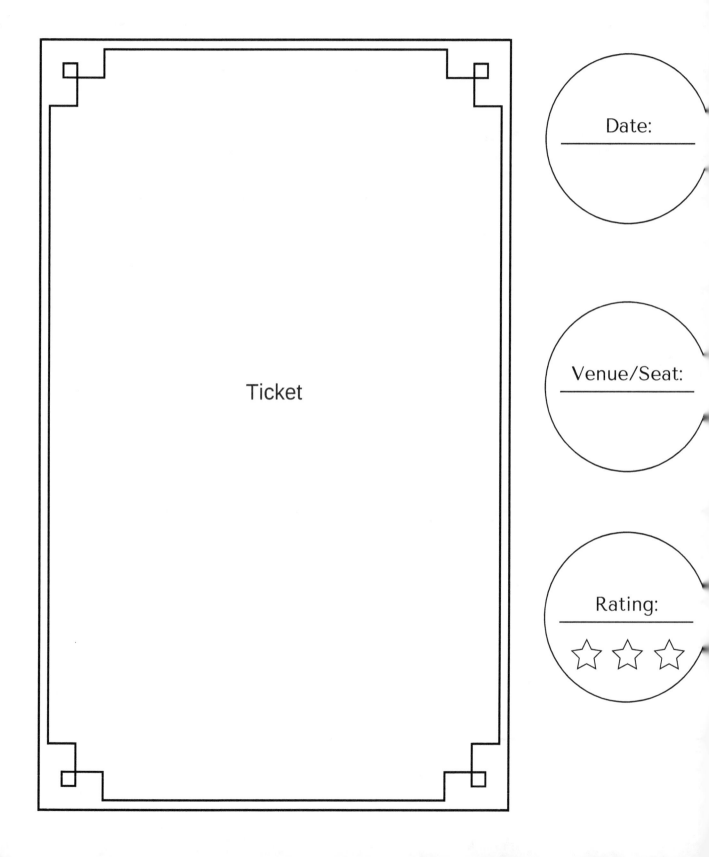

Ticket

Date:

Venue/Seat:

Rating:

Who I was with: _____

_____

_____

Awesomeness: _____

_____

_____

_____

Play List: _____

_____

_____

_____

_____

_____

_____

_____

Concert:

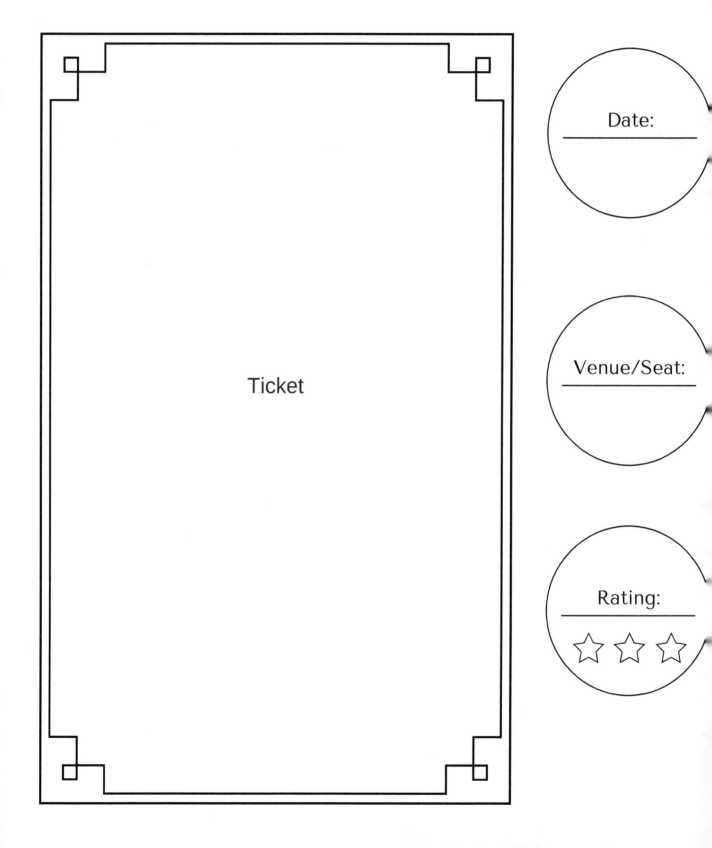

Ticket

Date:

Venue/Seat:

Rating:

Who I was with: _____

_____

_____

Awesomeness: _____

_____

_____

_____

Play List: _____

_____

_____

_____

_____

_____

_____

_____

Favorite Memories

Favorite Concert Venue:

_____

_____

_____

_____

_____

Favorite Concert Food:

_____

_____

_____

_____

_____

Favorite Concert So Far:

_____

_____

_____

_____

_____

Best Concert Experience So Far:

_____

_____

_____

_____

_____

_____

_____

_____

_____

_____

_____

Concert:

Ticket

Date:

Venue/Seat:

Rating:

Who I was with: _____

_____

_____

Awesomeness: _____

_____

_____

_____

Play List: _____

_____

_____

_____

_____

_____

_____

_____

Concert:

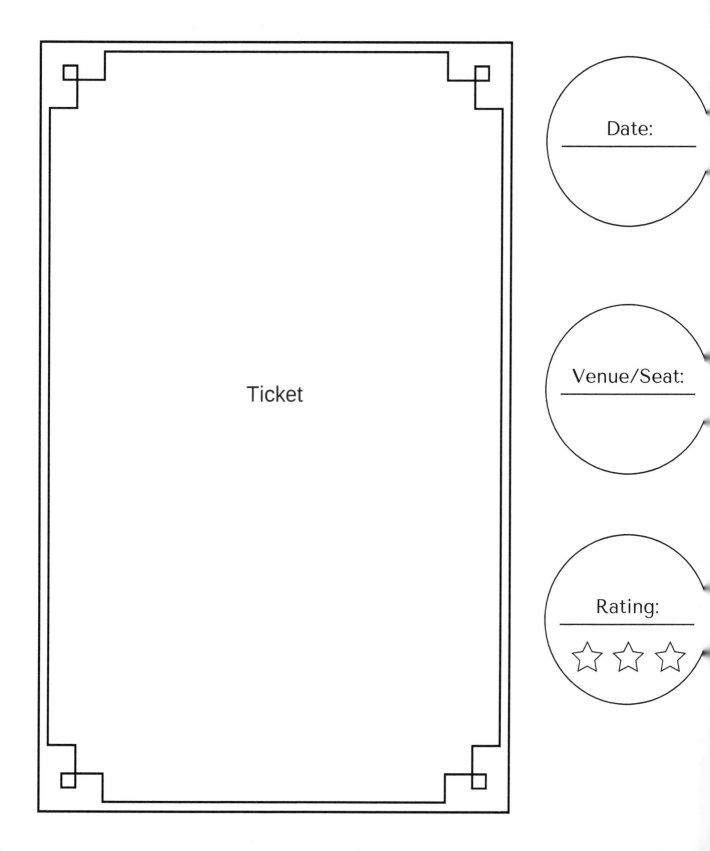

Ticket

Date:

Venue/Seat:

Rating:

Who I was with: _____

_____

_____

Awesomeness: _____

_____

_____

_____

Play List: _____

_____

_____

_____

_____

_____

_____

_____

Concert:

Ticket

Date:

Venue/Seat:

Rating:

Who I was with: _____

_____

_____

Awesomeness: _____

_____

_____

_____

Play List: _____

_____

_____

_____

_____

_____

_____

_____

Concert:

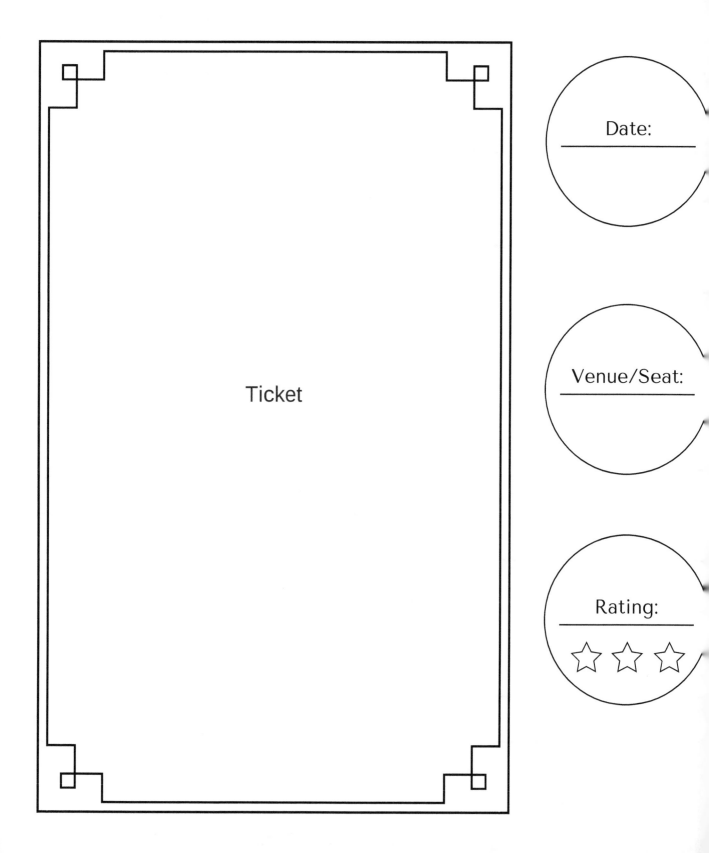

Ticket

Date:

Venue/Seat:

Rating:

Who I was with: _____

_____

_____

Awesomeness: _____

_____

_____

_____

Play List: _____

_____

_____

_____

_____

_____

_____

_____

Concert:

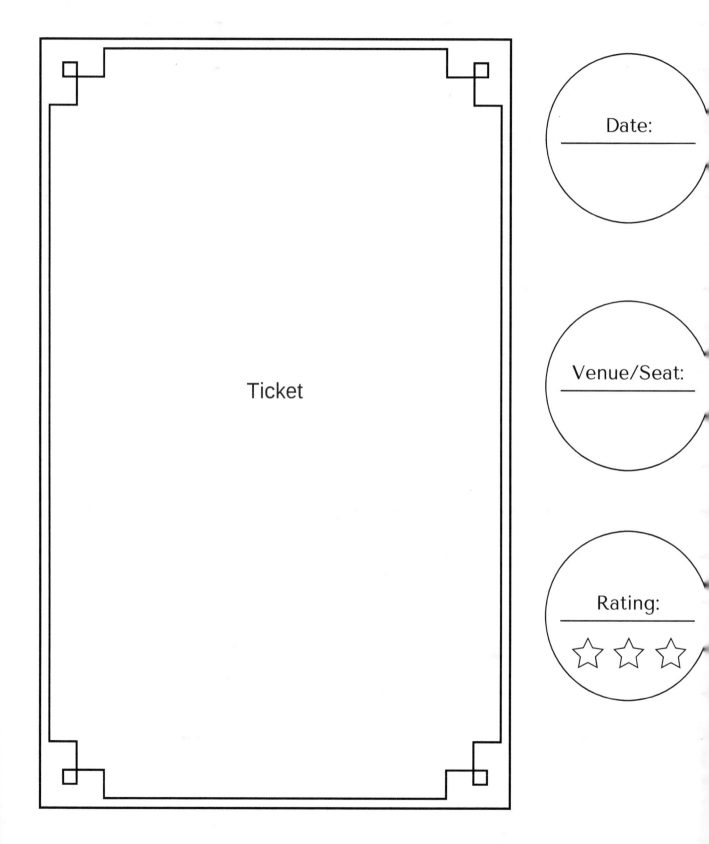

Ticket

Date:

Venue/Seat:

Rating:

Who I was with: _____

_____

_____

Awesomeness: _____

_____

_____

_____

Play List: _____

_____

_____

_____

_____

_____

_____

_____

Concert:

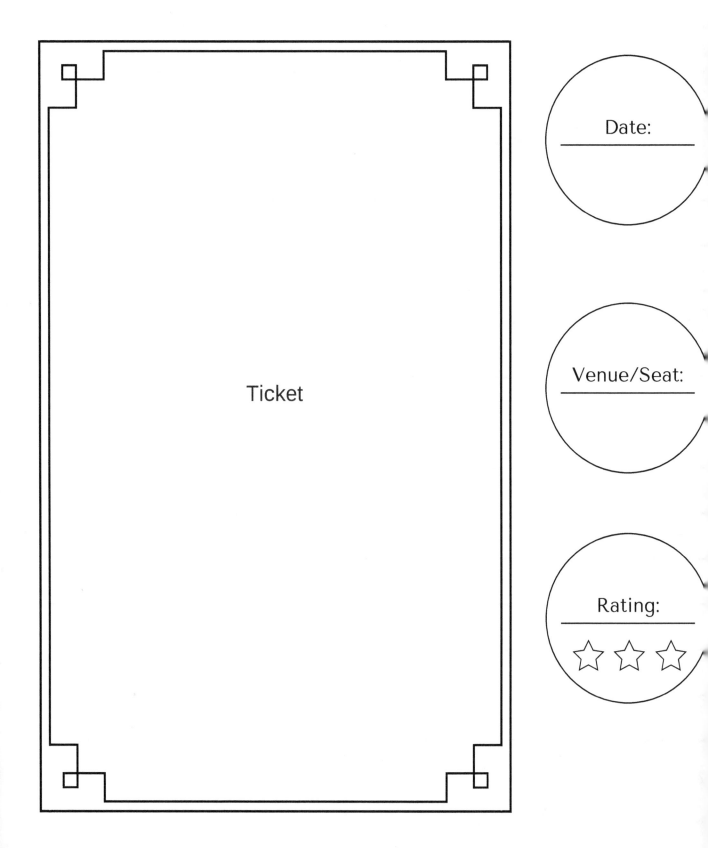

Ticket

Date:

Venue/Seat:

Rating:

Who I was with: _____

_____

_____

Awesomeness: _____

_____

_____

_____

Play List: _____

_____

_____

_____

_____

_____

_____

_____

Concert:

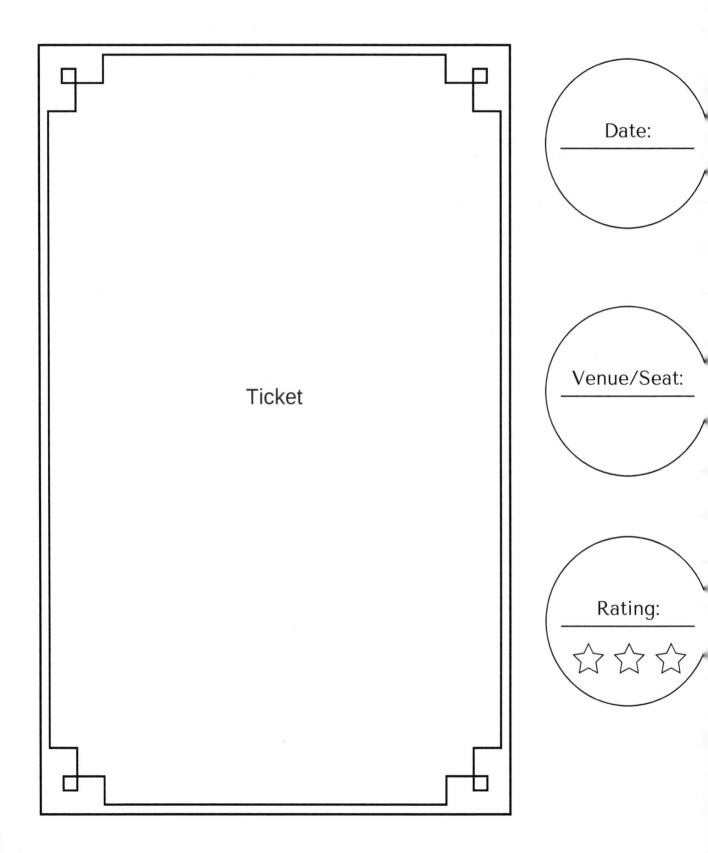

Ticket

Date:

Venue/Seat:

Rating:

Who I was with: _____

_____

_____

Awesomeness: _____

_____

_____

_____

Play List: _____

_____

_____

_____

_____

_____

_____

_____

Concert:

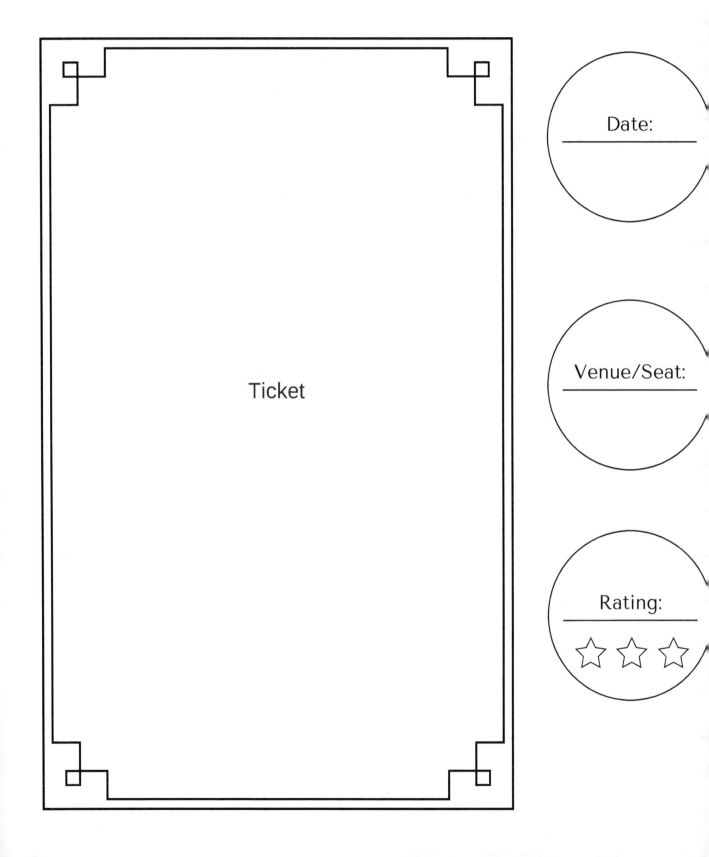

Ticket

Date:

Venue/Seat:

Rating:

Who I was with: _____

_____

_____

Awesomeness: _____

_____

_____

_____

Play List: _____

_____

_____

_____

_____

_____

_____

_____

Concert:

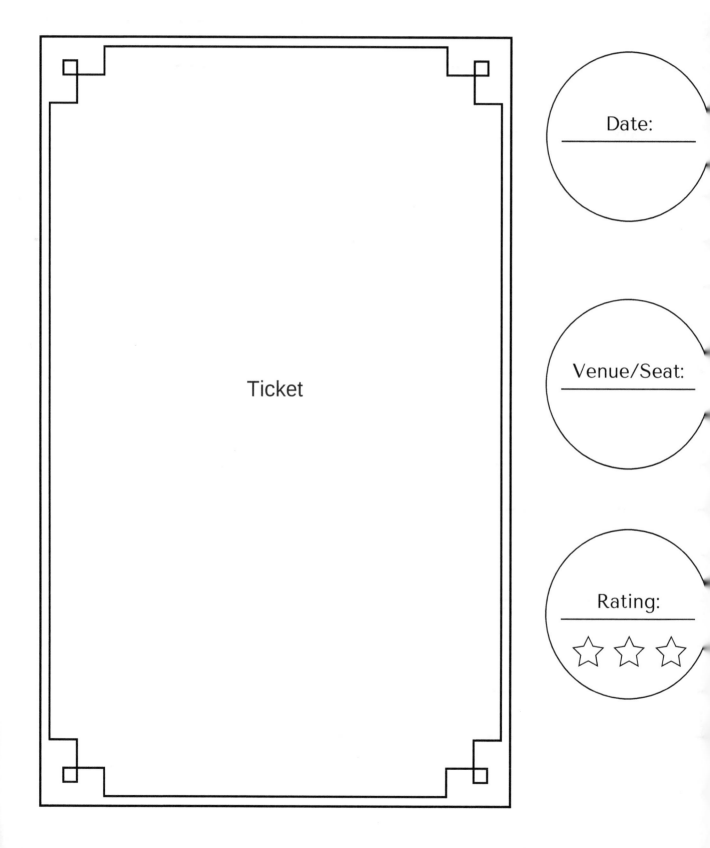

Ticket

Date:

Venue/Seat:

Rating:

Who I was with: _____

_____

_____

Awesomeness: _____

_____

_____

_____

Play List: _____

_____

_____

_____

_____

_____

_____

_____

Concert:

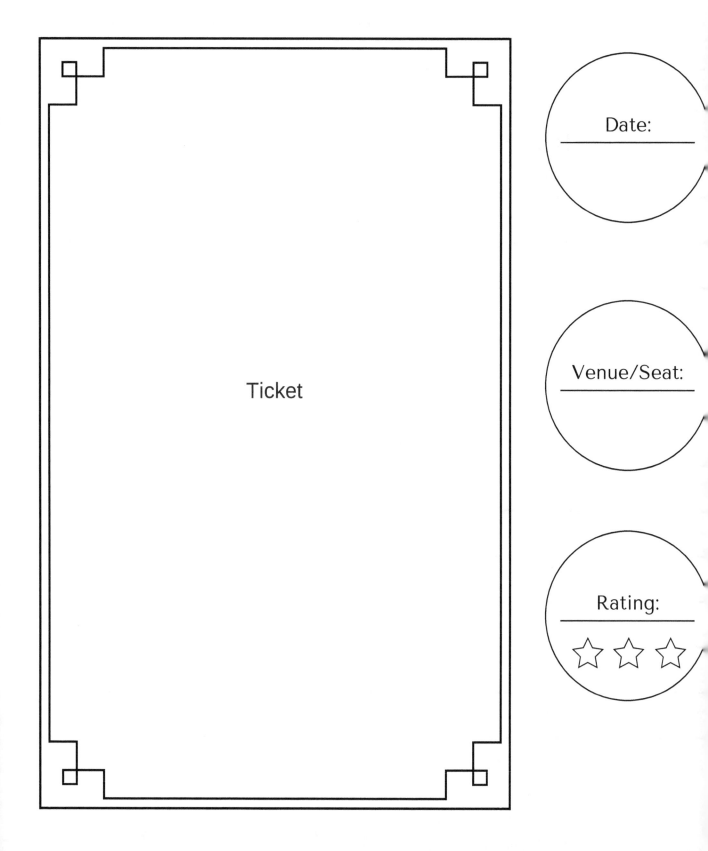

Ticket

Date:

Venue/Seat:

Rating:

Who I was with: _____

_____

_____

Awesomeness: _____

_____

_____

_____

Play List: _____

_____

_____

_____

_____

_____

_____

_____

_____

Concert:

Ticket

Date:

Venue/Seat:

Rating:

Who I was with: _____

_____

_____

Awesomeness: _____

_____

_____

_____

Play List: _____

_____

_____

_____

_____

_____

_____

_____

Concert:

Ticket

Date:

Venue/Seat:

Rating:

Who I was with: _____

_____

_____

Awesomeness: _____

_____

_____

_____

Play List: _____

_____

_____

_____

_____

_____

_____

_____

Concert:

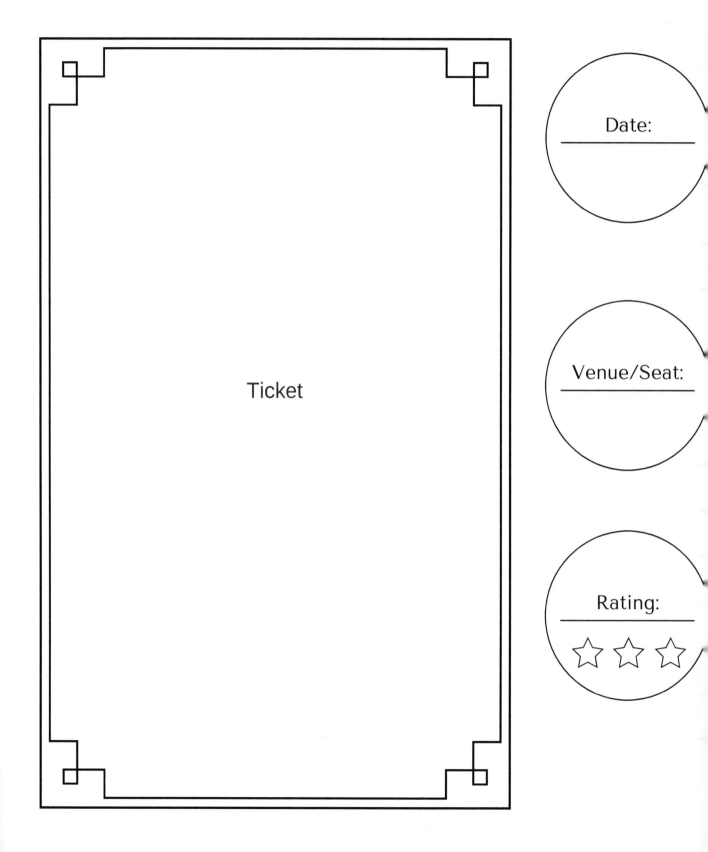

Ticket

Date:

Venue/Seat:

Rating:

Who I was with: _____

_____

_____

Awesomeness: _____

_____

_____

_____

Play List: _____

_____

_____

_____

_____

_____

_____

_____

Concert:

Ticket

Date:

Venue/Seat:

Rating:

Who I was with: _____

_____

_____

Awesomeness: _____

_____

_____

_____

Play List: _____

_____

_____

_____

_____

_____

_____

_____

Favorite Memories

Favorite Concert Venue:

_____

_____

_____

_____

_____

Favorite Concert Food:

_____

_____

_____

_____

_____

Favorite Concert So Far:

_____

_____

_____

_____

_____

Best Concert Experience So Far:

_____

_____

_____

_____

_____

_____

_____

_____

_____

_____

_____

_____

Concert:

Ticket

Date:

Venue/Seat:

Rating:

Who I was with: _____

_____

_____

Awesomeness: _____

_____

_____

_____

Play List: _____

_____

_____

_____

_____

_____

_____

_____

Concert:

Ticket

Date:

Venue/Seat:

Rating:

Who I was with: _____

_____

_____

Awesomeness: _____

_____

_____

_____

Play List: _____

_____

_____

_____

_____

_____

_____

_____

_____

Concert:

Ticket

Date:

Venue/Seat:

Rating:

Who I was with: _____

_____

_____

Awesomeness: _____

_____

_____

_____

Play List: _____

_____

_____

_____

_____

_____

_____

_____

Concert:

Ticket

Date:

Venue/Seat:

Rating:

Who I was with: _____

_____

_____

Awesomeness: _____

_____

_____

_____

Play List: _____

_____

_____

_____

_____

_____

_____

_____

_____

Concert:

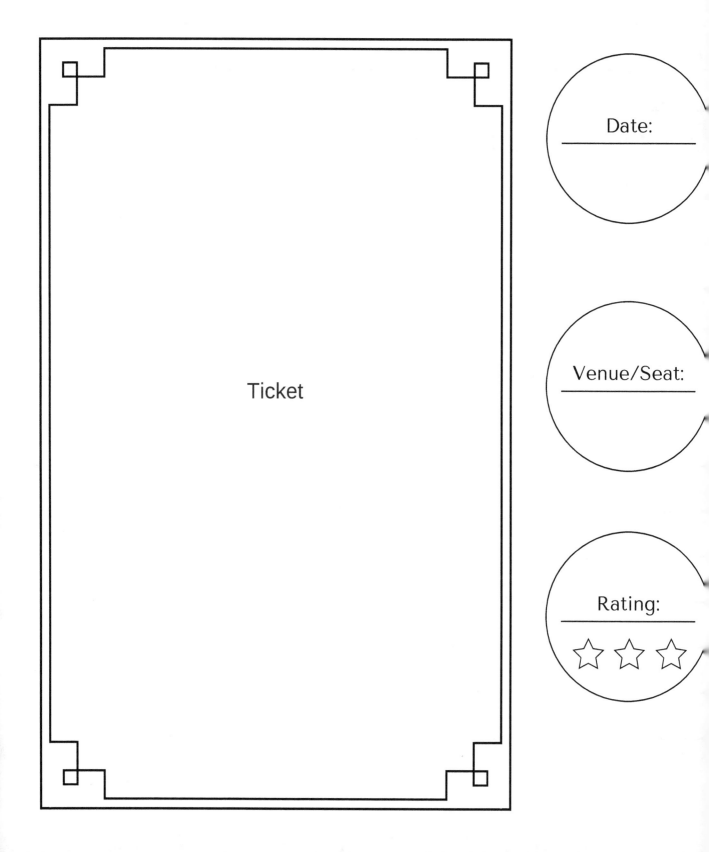

Ticket

Date:

Venue/Seat:

Rating:

Who I was with: _____

_____

_____

Awesomeness: _____

_____

_____

_____

Play List: _____

_____

_____

_____

_____

_____

_____

_____

Concert:

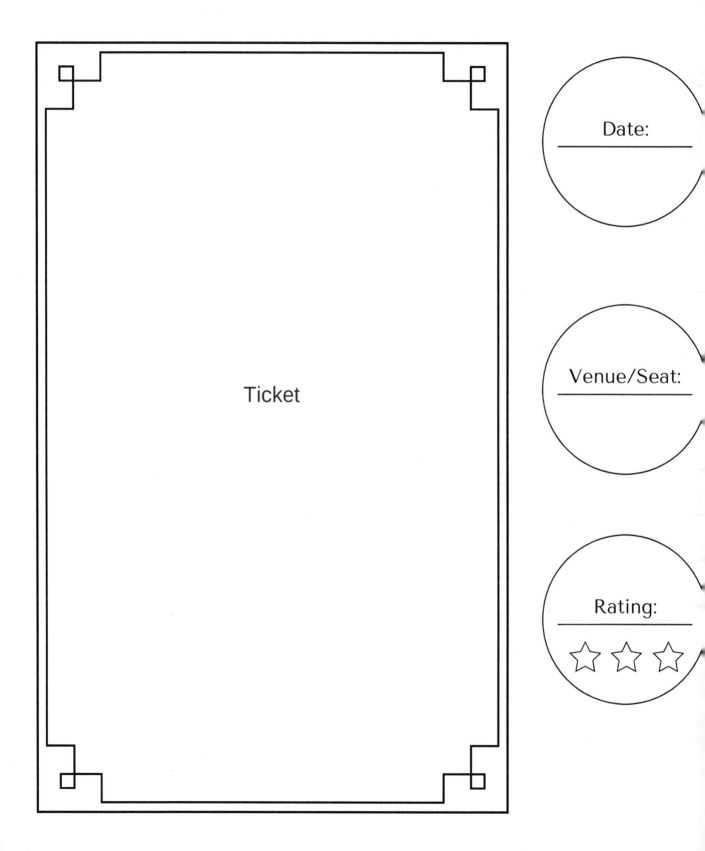

Ticket

Date:

Venue/Seat:

Rating:

Who I was with: _____

_____

_____

Awesomeness: _____

_____

_____

_____

Play List: _____

_____

_____

_____

_____

_____

_____

_____

Concert:

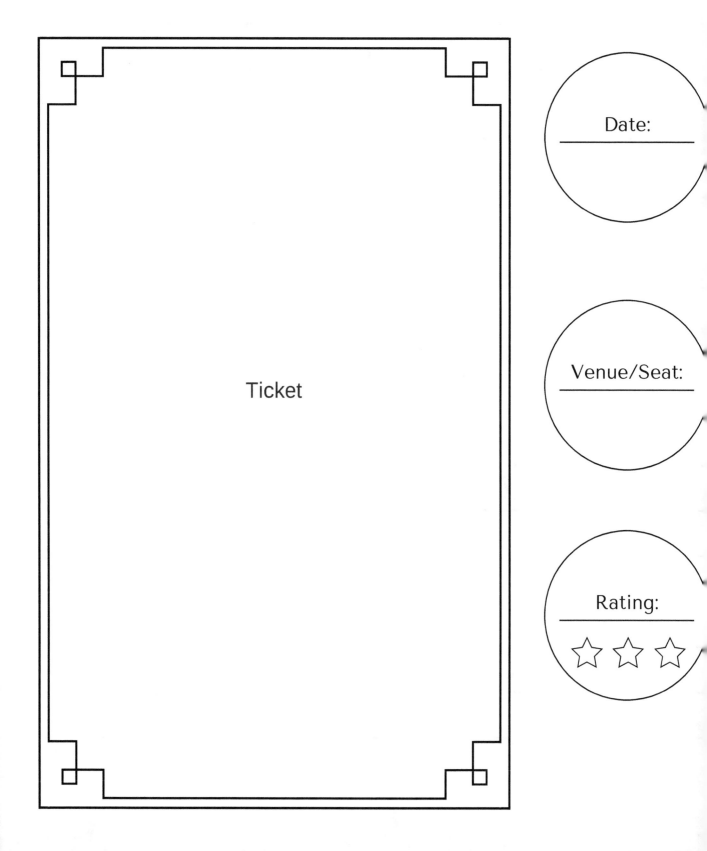

Ticket

Date:
_____

Venue/Seat:
_____

Rating:
_____
☆ ☆ ☆

Who I was with: _____

_____

_____

Awesomeness: _____

_____

_____

_____

Play List: _____

_____

_____

_____

_____

_____

_____

_____

_____

Concert:

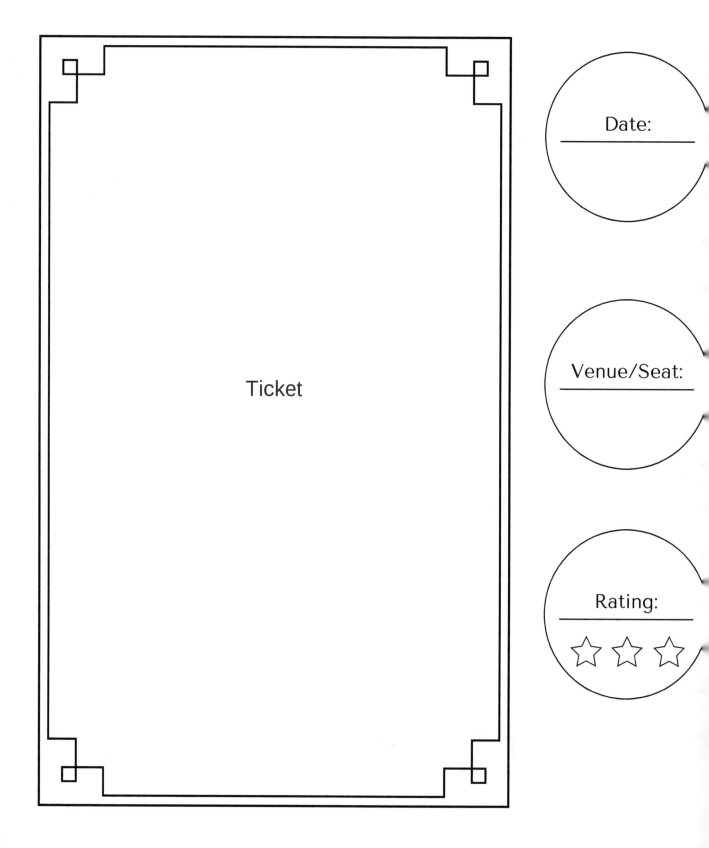

Ticket

Date:

Venue/Seat:

Rating:

Who I was with: _____

_____

_____

Awesomeness: _____

_____

_____

_____

Play List: _____

_____

_____

_____

_____

_____

_____

_____

Concert:

Ticket

Date:

Venue/Seat:

Rating:

Who I was with: _____

_____

_____

Awesomeness: _____

_____

_____

_____

Play List: _____

_____

_____

_____

_____

_____

_____

_____

_____

Concert:

Ticket

Date:

Venue/Seat:

Rating:

Who I was with: _____

_____

_____

Awesomeness: _____

_____

_____

_____

Play List: _____

_____

_____

_____

_____

_____

_____

_____

Concert:

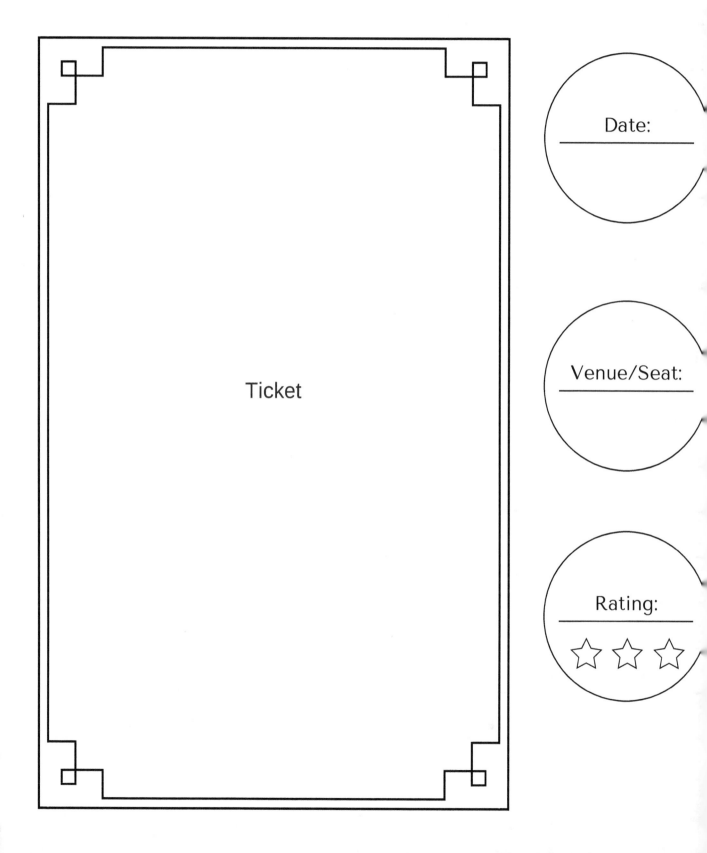

Ticket

Date:

Venue/Seat:

Rating:

Who I was with: _____

_____

_____

Awesomeness: _____

_____

_____

_____

Play List: _____

_____

_____

_____

_____

_____

_____

_____

Concert:

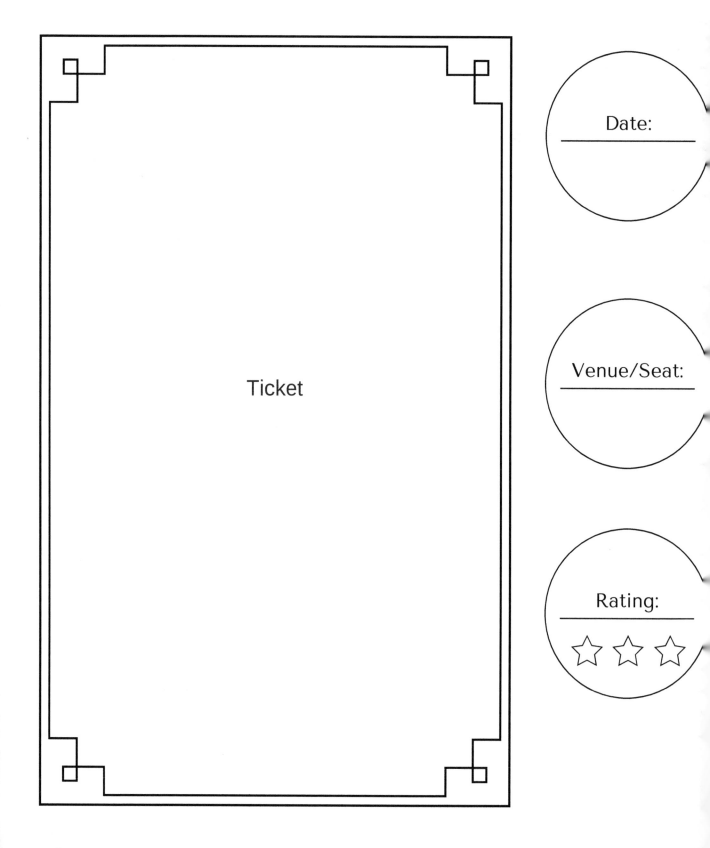

Ticket

Date:

Venue/Seat:

Rating:

Who I was with: _____

_____

_____

Awesomeness: _____

_____

_____

_____

Play List: _____

_____

_____

_____

_____

_____

_____

_____

Concert:

Ticket

Date:

Venue/Seat:

Rating:

Who I was with: _____

_____

_____

Awesomeness: _____

_____

_____

_____

Play List: _____

_____

_____

_____

_____

_____

_____

_____

Concert:

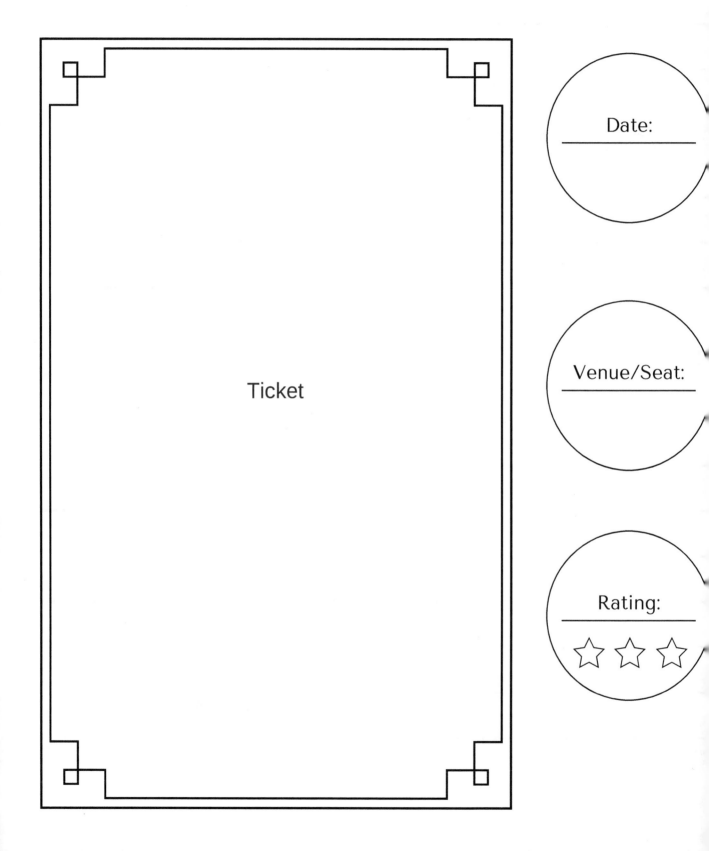

Ticket

Date:

Venue/Seat:

Rating:

Who I was with: _____

_____

_____

Awesomeness: _____

_____

_____

_____

Play List: _____

_____

_____

_____

_____

_____

_____

_____

_____

How to Attach your Ticket Stub to the Page

You can attach your ticket stub in a number of ways:
1. use a fastener like a brad, which enables you to remove the ticket easily so you can see the front and the back.
2. foam mounting tape will raise your ticket up off the page.
3. glue dot are quick and easy. Try "mini glue dots."
4. photo tabs let you "click and stick."

Check the scrapbooking supplies in a hobby or craft store or even many drug stores or big retail stores for multiple types of fixatives that will allow you to stick your ticket without harming it.

You can also go to Amazon and type in "scrapbooking tape" and you will find many options for affixing your ticket to the page.